Witley Court

Roger White

Introduction

Once one of England's great country houses, Witley Court was largely gutted by fire in 1937. The owner, Sir Herbert Smith, decided not to rebuild but to put the estate up for sale. Witley was never lived in again and was subsequently stripped and abandoned. Yet, as a ruin, it remains deeply evocative. Today it offers a rare opportunity to see the bones of a mansion that has grown over the centuries, from a substantial Jacobean house, based on a medieval manor house, through expansion under the first Baron Foley and his son in the 1720s and 1730s to the addition of two massive porticos by Regency architect John Nash. It finally reached its peak of grandeur in the 1850s with the extensive remodelling commissioned by the first earl of Dudley from the architect Samuel Daukes.

Lord Dudley's immense wealth, generated largely by his industrial enterprises in the West Midlands, enabled his family to live an extraordinarily opulent life. It also funded the creation of an ornate formal garden at Witley designed by William Andrews Nesfield, the leading garden designer of his day. An army of servants was involved in servicing the property and family, further swollen during the lavish house parties attended by the prince of Wales (later King Edward VII) and his circle.

The south parterre has recently been recreated to give an idea of its former Victorian glory, and restoration of the east parterre is also underway. The Perseus and Andromeda fountain – one of the grandest in Europe – has been restored to working order. The formal gardens are complemented by the surrounding landscape of parkland, woodland and wilderness gardens. The ensemble is completed by the Georgian parish church (not owned by English Heritage), which boasts one of the finest interiors of its period in the country.

Below: Rachel, countess of Dudley, dressed as Queen Esther for a ball held in 1897 to celebrate Queen Victoria's Diamond Jubilee. According to the Morning Post, her costume was 'embroidered in real dull gold' and 'studded with amethysts, turquoises and pearls'

Facing page: Looking through the massive Ionic columns of John Nash's south portico into the saloon beyond

Tour

The recently restored gardens at Witley Court provide a dramatic setting for the ruins of this sprawling mansion – once one of the grandest in England. Though stripped of most of its fittings after the 1937 fire, the visitor can still gain a sense of the opulence and scale of the 19th-century interior. It is also possible to see earlier layers of the building's history laid bare by the fire.

FOLLOWING THE TOUR

The tour begins on the north side of the Front Pool, and follows the path by the lake to the main house. Visitors can then explore the accessible ground-floor rooms of the house before progressing to the formal gardens to the south and east. The small numbered plans in the margins highlight the key points in the tour.

THE SETTING

Witley Court and church sit on the far side of the lake known as Front Pool, which was originally formed in the 18th century by damming a stream. Visitors would once have reached the house by a causeway across the lake, and later by the carriage drive which you can see in front of the buildings. The ornamental woodland known as the wilderness was originally developed at some point between 1772 and 1794, with walks laid out along the banks of Front Pool and the Shrawley Brook, which flows out of it. The planting was predominantly deciduous, with oaks, sweet chestnut and beech. In the early 19th century a new curving drive was created through the woodland and across the north front of the house, with lodges where it met the public road, probably designed by John Nash or G S Repton (these are shown on the 1828 Ordnance Survey map). The lodges were replaced in 1888 by the existing lodges in French Second Empire style, designed by Henry Rowe of Worcester. In the 1870s and 1880s rhododendron walks were introduced and the valley below the dam was extensively planted with American ornamental trees and plants, together with a profusion of spring-flowering bulbs and shrubs. Below the dam a footbridge took the path across the Shrawley Brook, reinstated in timber and stone in 1999. This extensive area of woodland was separated from the house in the sales that followed the fire of 1937, with many of the fine mature trees being felled. Altogether, about half the wilderness was cleared to form paddocks. Work is now under way to replace the sycamore woodland that has grown up since then with the original mixed woodland and ornamental planting, together with new footpaths and viewing points.

Above: Witley Court and Great Witley Church seen from the north across Front Pool

Facing page: The north portico, with its paving of pink granite and black and white marble, photographed before the fire of 1937

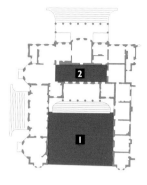

❶ FORECOURT

The appearance of the house as it now stands is largely the result of an extensive remodelling in the mid-19th century. Its bones however, are those of the Jacobean house built between about 1610 and 1620, which already had twin towers and wings extending to the left and right on the north side. Impressive though it now is, until the early 19th century the composition must have looked even more imposing from this side, since it was further extended to the left and right by a pair of large, 18th-century service wings and arcaded screen walls. These were demolished by John Nash, the celebrated architect to the Prince Regent, who also added the portico of six massive Ionic columns to the centre. He might have given the brick house a coating of white stucco, which was then replaced, in the 1850s, by much more expensive Bath stone to match the portico. It is possible to see where the stone has come away in places to reveal the original Jacobean brick construction.

The Victorian transformation, designed by Samuel Daukes for the first earl of Dudley, gave the house the Italianate look made fashionable ten years earlier in the 1840s by Osborne House on the Isle of Wight, built for Queen Victoria. Daukes's internal reconstruction of the left-hand wing, from four floors to three, meant that the existing windows were at the wrong level, so on the courtyard side they were blocked up but given false glazing to correspond to the wing opposite.

❷ ENTRANCE HALL

The site of the present entrance hall has been the heart of the house at Witley since medieval times, when the great hall of the manor house was located here. (The remains of the early 14th-century vaulted undercroft survive beneath

Right and facing page: Views of the entrance hall looking west – one showing the hall as it is now, and the other as it was in 1920

KEY

❶ Staircase leading to the first floor

❷ Archway leading to the west wing first-floor rooms

❸ Gallery landing with state apartments leading off and carton pierre decoration

❹ Entrance leading to the north portico

❺ Doorway leading to the saloon

❻ Supports for the balcony

the modern concrete floor.) This was succeeded by the hall of the Jacobean house, which in turn became the entrance hall in successive remodellings. Here visitors would have been greeted by the staff or, if they were sufficiently important, by the owners themselves.

Nash was responsible for turning it into a double-height room, running between the dining room to the left and the main staircase, which rose beyond the blocked opening to the right; note its cast-iron frame. The hall received its final remodelling and redecoration in the 1850s. Victorian photographs show it furnished with 18th-century hall settees (probably from the earlier house), potted palms and plenty of 19th-century marble sculpture. The staircase was an 'imperial' one, with a central flight which divided at a half-landing and returned in two flights to reach the balcony that ran around the hall at first-floor level. This in turn gave access to bedrooms and also to the picture gallery in the west wing (see pages 8–9). Immediately beyond the staircase was the large top-lit kitchen.

In comparison with many of the other interiors, the hall decoration was restrained, with simple panelling on the walls (executed in 'carton pierre', a form of strengthened papier mâché popular in the Victorian period), and a deeply beamed ceiling. Almost all the decoration was destroyed by the fire, but sections of the panelling survive to the right of the door opposite the entrance. To the left of the same door is a blocked window with vertical mullion and horizontal transom in sandstone, a relic of the Jacobean house and a reminder that until about 1730 the centre block of the house was only one room thick; hidden behind panelling for 200 years, the fire brought it to light again. On the inside of the north portico wall can be seen the supports for the balcony.

Above: A surviving section of carton pierre decoration. Made from a mixture containing shredded paper, glue and flour, it was an early way to mass-produce decorative mouldings

Behind the Scenes

In its heyday Witley Court was a classic example of how a great Victorian country house functioned. 'Below stairs', the basement (really the ground floor) extended under the entire house, although parts of the area under the west wing were inaccessible. It was a labyrinth of mostly small rooms, with the main service passage running from the large square kitchen immediately behind the grand staircase, to the butler's pantry beneath the dining room on the east front. Beneath the steps to the east parterre was a tiled room, probably used as a dairy, while under the saloon was the housekeeper's room. A further level below the housekeeper's room housed the boilers.

A very extensive area to the west of the main house was also given over to services of various kinds, including servants' hall and servants' bedrooms – three courtyards ending in the coach houses. Next to the stable yard stood a gigantic coal stack, maintained at about 1,500 tonnes, which fed five hot-water boilers and the dozens of fireplaces in the house. A track with a small trolley in a tunnel connected the coal stack to a cellar beneath the house. The heating system would consume as much as 30 tonnes of coal per day – Dudley coal, of course, brought from the Black Country by barge to Shrawley on the river Severn and carried the remaining four miles by the horses and carts of tenant farmers.

Below: Housemaids in their day dresses, and a male servant in an apron taking tea in the entrance hall. This photograph must have been taken during the family's absence – the furniture in the background is covered with dust sheets

3 WEST TOWER

To the left of the portico wall a well-preserved early 17th-century doorcase leads into the west tower. In the 17th and 18th centuries this and the corresponding east tower contained staircases, vestiges of which remain between the second and third floors. More of the carton pierre decoration can be seen here and also laths to support plaster on the walls. In the Victorian house the entrance hall level of the west tower contained a room from which servants kept watch for visitors approaching up the forecourt. Both towers are now internally braced with concrete ring-frames to prevent collapse.

4 WEST WING ROOMS

The west wing originally contained the Jacobean long gallery on its upper floor, which was altered

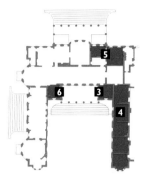

5 SITTING ROOMS

The Red Room and adjoining Red Sitting Room were part of the sequence of rooms added across the south side of the Jacobean house in the 1730s, and would have been used as private sitting rooms. The site of the Red Room was originally a short wing projecting from the south-west corner of the Jacobean house. Surrounding the 19th-century doorway in the right-hand wall of the Red Sitting Room is the outline of the outer side of a 17th-century window, while in the adjacent corner are finely laid stone quoins (or cornerstones) – both indications that this was once an outside wall. Above were bedrooms reserved for important guests, especially royalty.

6 EAST TOWER

In the Jacobean house, this was another staircase tower. In the early 19th century the stairs were removed and the space at ground level was remodelled as a circular vestibule, making it possible to enter the library in the east wing (the predecessor to the ballroom) without going through the dining room – the blocked door can be seen in the east wall to your right. On Victorian plans, this room is labelled as the 'library'. In the 1937 fire, which started in the bakery in the cellars directly below this room, the tower acted as a kind of flue, and fanned the flames.

Left: The picture gallery in about 1882, epitomizing the fully furnished Victorian look
Below: *The intimate Red Sitting Room in 1920. The alcoves can still be seen today*

in the 19th century to contain a top-lit picture gallery – possibly by John Nash, who created such galleries at Buckingham Palace and Attingham Hall in Shropshire. In addition to some fine French, Italian and Flemish paintings (and, it is said, a J M W Turner view of the Grand Canal in Venice), old photographs show much standard mid-Victorian upholstered seating as well as reproduction 'Boulle' (French-style furniture inlaid with brass and tortoiseshell), that would have chimed with the French style of decoration. The wing as a whole was also known as the Bachelor Wing, with bedrooms on the ground floor for unmarried male guests, since segregated sleeping arrangements were the rule in Victorian country houses. A corridor along the rear of the wing enabled family and guests to walk under cover to services in the adjoining church.

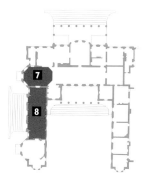

Right: An illustration of a Victorian ball in progress, from 1847. The décor is similar to that at Witley

Below: The dining room in 1920, as remodelled in the 1850s for entertaining small groups of guests and friends

Facing page: The ballroom with its gilded plasterwork and crystal chandeliers. The Green Salon to the north can be glimpsed through the open doors at the far end

7 DINING ROOM

Until the fire, a wall with tall double doors divided the hall from the dining room. Here the owners would dine on their own or with relatively small gatherings of guests and friends; for larger, more formal dinners the ballroom or even the picture gallery would be used. Beneath the dining room was a spacious butler's pantry, from which the room was serviced at meal times via a small adjoining servery and staircase; the food was brought at the lower level from the main kitchen on the opposite side of the house.

In plan the dining room was an elongated octagon, originally formed at the beginning of the 19th century by John Nash, who seems to have decorated it in an 'Etruscan' style based on the decoration of Greek and Etruscan vases. Soon after the first earl of Dudley came into his inheritance in 1848, it was completely remodelled in the then fashionable Louis XV style, with the walls divided into round-arched panels in which doors alternated with great sheets of mirror glass. The moulded decorations were of carton pierre, some of which survives on the walls. A photograph of 1920 shows a white marble

chimneypiece, Victorian dining table and chairs, and elegant early 19th-century side tables on which were placed ornate candelabra. The windows overlook the east parterre garden with the Flora fountain at its centre.

8 BALLROOM

The ballroom, again decorated in Louis XV style, was undoubtedly the most magnificent room in the house, 21m (69ft) long and extending almost the full length of the north-east wing. The ceiling, too, was higher than those of the other reception rooms, making it possible to light the room with eight enormous crystal chandeliers. As part of the general remodelling by Lord Dudley in the 1850s, the ballroom replaced an equally splendid library and was created to accommodate glittering balls, dinners and other large-scale social gatherings. On these occasions the innumerable flickering candles would have caught the gold leaf on the sumptuous plaster ornament of the walls and ceiling. At Christmas it is said that the second Lord Dudley had the ballroom tree hung with precious jewellery, from which female guests chose before they left the house.

The fire of 1937 was particularly intense here, revealing the rivetted steel girders that supported the floor above and charring the window timbers.

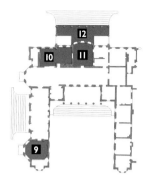

9 GREEN SALON

At the opposite end of the ballroom to the dining room, the Green Salon was another octagonal room, perhaps used by those taking a break from the dancing next door. It was also used by Lady Rachel, countess of Dudley, as her private day room. Beyond it was a small anteroom, which contained a staircase descending to a sunken bath in the basement. This was probably a relic of the Foley era – in the 18th century, cold baths were often recommended for medical reasons.

10 DRAWING ROOM

In the 1730s, the range of rooms on the south side of the house, which included this drawing room, the saloon and the sitting rooms (see page 9), was added to the Jacobean house. On the east wall of the drawing room is a chimneystack that was once on the outer wall. In the 19th century the drawing room was created out of two smaller 18th-century rooms, when the dividing wall was replaced with a pair of Ionic columns. The resulting room, with its gilded Louis XV-style panelling, was spacious but low-ceilinged. All the decoration in this room was destroyed in the fire, but there are remains of two Victorian fire grates in the rooms above at first-floor level.

11 SALOON

The bow-fronted saloon is at the centre of the south, or garden, front of the mansion. In the 18th century it would have been an important room for socializing, although the addition of the massive portico outside must have made it rather dark. In Victorian times it was used mainly as a passage room leading to the garden. Some of the carton pierre decoration from that period survives.

12 SOUTH PORTICO

Like the portico on the north front, through which visitors entered the house, the south portico was added by John Nash in the early 19th century. Eight columns wide and two deep, it is probably the biggest of any country house in Britain. The floor was originally paved in a design (thought to be of the signs of the Zodiac) in pink sandstone and black and white marble, of which there are remains between some of the pillars. Above the door from the saloon, the elaborate decoration was recarved in 1993 as a result of a private donation from Miss Barbara Mapstone of Cheltenham. The great columns of the portico frame a fine view over the formal gardens.

Right: A photograph of the drawing room from 1920. This room was formed in the 1850s from two smaller rooms, and is decorated in the French Rococo style

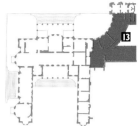

🄳 SERVICE COURTYARDS

Some time in the 18th century, a long narrow range containing servants' rooms was built on the west side of the house. The kitchen, which had previously been in the basement of the east wing, was moved to its position immediately to the west of the main staircase at this time. This range was then incorporated into a complex of three courts created in the early 19th century by John Nash, which included the stable court with its attractive clock tower, recently restored.

In the mid-19th century a long curving wing was added by the architect Samuel Daukes to connect the south-west corner of the house to the enormous new conservatory. Although only the outer wall now remains, it contained the servants' hall and other service rooms at the lower level, with the nursery, schoolroom and governess's accommodation above. None of the service courtyards is yet open to the public, but it is possible to look into them through the lower windows at this point.

The service courtyard behind the curved wing, which was known as the Kitchen Court or Back Court, was the usual access to the house for servants and tradesmen and also, on a day-to-day basis, for members of the Dudley family. It was flanked by arcades which screened such subsidiary rooms as the gun room and game larder on the south and the laundry, drying rooms and kitchen maids' rooms on the north. A long passage led from the laundry out to the drying grounds, probably to ensure that the laundry maids were shielded from the attentions of the stable lads, for between the two lay the stable court (latterly including garage space for seven cars, workshops and an engine room) and an outer court with harness rooms and coach houses. The whole service area was unaffected by the 1937 fire but was stripped out and allowed to fall into ruin in the 1940s.

Above: The south front at Witley Court, with the restored Perseus and Andromeda fountain and recreated south parterre
Below: The laundry staff in the service courtyard

Above: The Victorian conservatory had a curved glass roof – a technique used for the Crystal Palace a few years earlier in 1851

Below: The twin sons of the second earl of Dudley, in the conservatory with their sister Alexandra (named after her godmother, Queen Alexandra)

▣ MICHELANGELO PAVILION

At the end of the curved service wing, entry into the conservatory was provided by the elegant Michelangelo Pavilion, so-called because Daukes based its design on that of the Capitoline Museum in Rome, designed by the architect, sculptor and painter Michelangelo Buonarroti in about 1539. Inside are a tessellated floor and niches for statues.

▣ CONSERVATORY

The conservatory, sometimes known as the orangery, was one of the largest to be found in any English country house: 13 bays long by 5 deep. In the late 1850s it replaced a smaller detached conservatory in this position designed by Nash. Sheets of plate glass were fitted directly into the stonework of the arches without conventional window frames (fragments of glass can still be seen), while the enormous interior was spanned by a great curved glass roof. Inside was a marble floor, some of which remains, and raised beds with stone edgings. The stone baskets of flowers on the rear wall were carved by the Scottish sculptor James Forsyth (1827–1910), who also carried out much of the other carving

around the house, while the stone block near the centre once supported an ornamental urn. Exotic plants such as palm trees were kept alive with help from the conservatory's self-contained heating system, fuelled by the Dudleys' own coal. Although it escaped the fire, reusable materials such as the lead and plate glass were afterwards stripped out and sold, leaving a roofless shell. Of the planting, only the large camellia on the rear wall remains from before 1937, but additional camellias have now been added, together with vines.

▣ LOUIS XVI COURT

Fruit trees were trained up the walls of this sheltered area. The niche in the far wall contained a statue now at Harlaxton Manor, Lincolnshire. Behind the screen wall was the vast coal store, kept stocked at a level of 1,500 tonnes, since at peak times the mansion's elaborate heating system consumed as much as 30 tonnes a day. The coal was transported by water from the Black Country to Stourport-on-Severn, and then by cart to Witley, where two or three coalmen were employed to sort it by grade for fireplaces and furnaces.

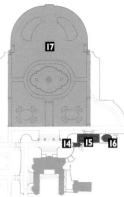

17 SOUTH PARTERRE AND PERSEUS AND ANDROMEDA FOUNTAIN

When, in the 1850s, the earl of Dudley had the house remodelled in the Italianate style, he called in the leading garden designer William Andrews Nesfield to provide an appropriately grand setting. This was implemented between 1854 and 1860. In front of Nash's south portico Nesfield introduced a vast flight of steps, curving out to each side. At the foot is a pair of stone plinths which were originally surmounted by lions. From here a broad central path leads down to the large oval pool containing the spectacular Perseus and Andromeda fountain. The theme of the central sculptural group, which was carved in Portland stone by James Forsyth, is the classical myth of Perseus and Andromeda. Perseus, having obtained the head of Medusa with the help of his winged sandals and his helmet of invisibility, flies to the rescue of Andromeda; she has been chained to a rock by the sea god Poseidon, angry at the suggestion that she is more beautiful than the sea nymphs. A sea monster threatens to devour her, but Perseus gets there first and carries her off on the back of the winged horse

Pegasus. Rising out of the water to the left and right are two cupids riding dolphins, replicas based on photographs of the lost originals.

The engineers for the fountain were Easton & Co, who had worked on other Nesfield commissions at Holkham Hall in Norfolk and Castle Howard in Yorkshire. To supply the necessary water, 18,000 litres (4,000 gallons) were pumped from a nearby pool to a reservoir more than half a mile away and 30m (100ft) above the level of the house. The main jet, which shot from the sea monster's open mouth, is said to have

Above: The house and fountains in the 1880s, possibly at the time of the second earl's coming-of-age celebrations in 1888, as there is a large marquee to the east of the house

Below: One of the young twin sons of the second earl of Dudley, astride a sculpted lion that originally stood on the south portico steps

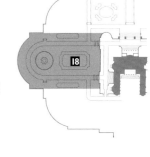

reached a height of 36m (120ft), and there were numerous subsidiary jets and sprays, as can be seen in early photographs. In its Victorian heyday the fountain played twice a week.

As first laid out, the fountain was surrounded by a pattern of formal borders, outlined by stone kerbs, and evergreens (Portuguese laurels, cypresses and yew) clipped into pyramids and cones, which have been reinstated by English Heritage. The lie of the land meant that the pattern could be appreciated from either the portico or the windows of the house. Beyond the pool a cross-terrace is terminated at each end by an elaborate stone pavilion with classical columns but a vaguely Hindu-style roof, designed by Nesfield, probably with input from Samuel Daukes. The continuation of the parterre to the south, where the ground slopes upwards again, is enclosed by a low semicircular balustrade and ha-ha, which separates the garden from what was the park (now farmland).

At the centre of the balustrade, on axis with the portico and fountain, was a set of magnificent gates in gilded wrought iron (see page 20), exhibited at the Paris Exhibition in 1862 and erected here to commemorate Queen Victoria's Silver Jubilee in the same year; these are now in Arizona. From the site of the gates there is a fine panorama of the house and church.

18 EAST PARTERRE

To the east of the house was a smaller garden containing a highly elaborate French-style parterre, which could be admired from the windows of the ballroom. It featured flowing designs laid out with box and filled with coloured gravels and flowers. This garden also contained clipped evergreens, flowering shrubs and ornamental bowls filled with flowers. To the right was a long guilloche, or ribbon of flowers.

The focal point when viewed from the house was a fountain of Flora, goddess of spring and of flowers, whose statue crowned the composition. She holds a cornucopia or horn, intended to jet water, and around her are four tritons (fish-tailed humans) blowing jets of water from conch shells. Smaller jets line the circumference of the basin. The original Flora statue was broken some years ago when an attempt was made to remove it, and the fountain as a whole has been badly vandalized. In Witley's heyday under the earls of Dudley, whenever there was a ball in progress, the windows would be thrown open and the gardens illuminated with hundreds of coloured lanterns.

Restoration began in 2005, with a donation from the Wolfson Trust, and following garden archaeology, recreation of the planting is being undertaken. It is hoped that funds will permit restoration of the fountain at a later date.

Left: Gardeners working in the east parterre in 1910

Facing page: The restored Perseus and Andromeda fountain, which was inaugurated by HRH the Prince of Wales in 2002

History of the Garden

Just as the house at Witley was extended and altered to serve changing tastes and fashions, so the gardens were developed by generations of owners. The early deer park, fields and orchards of the Jacobean mansion were replaced by an ornamental lake, formal parterres and the spectacular fountains, set within gardens that designer William Andrews Nesfield described as his 'monster work'.

Left: Perseus, astride the winged horse Pegasus, kills a sea monster – the south parterre fountain in full flow

THE EARLY GARDENS AT WITLEY COURT

Very little is known of the early gardens of Witley Court, although it can certainly be assumed that they were formal. Almost the only piece of evidence is a lost late 17th-century painting illustrated on page 25, which shows walled compartments on the slope below the south front. An estate map of 1732 (see page 28) shows the area to the south of this subdivided into fields, with an extensive deer park lying to the west, but by 1772 Isaac Taylor's map of Worcestershire shows the parkland extending to the south as well. The first Lord Foley also acquired land to the north so that an appropriately grand approach could be created on that side, with an axial causeway and bridge across Front Pool, formed by damming the Shrawley Brook. A formal avenue was laid out to the east, crossing a ravine by another causeway.

Between 1772 and 1794 an ornamental woodland known as the wilderness was developed north-east of the house, with walks laid out along the banks of Front Pool and Shrawley Brook. Ornamental plantations were also laid out to enhance the park. Thomas Foley VII, who owned Witley from 1793, called in John Nash to remodel the house. He probably also commissioned the leading landscape designer Humphry Repton to redesign its setting. On the south and east fronts the house was surrounded by a new raised terrace and simple flower beds, while on the north side the formal causeway was removed in favour of curving carriage drives leading out to the turnpike road. The park was extended east to include Warford Pool and, more generally, the condition of the land was improved by means of better drainage and the introduction of a herd of bullocks to eat the rushes.

NESFIELD AND THE CREATION OF THE FORMAL GARDENS

The most dramatic transformation of the setting of Witley Court came between 1854 and 1860, when the first earl of Dudley commissioned William Andrews Nesfield (1794–1881) to design new gardens that would complement the work on the mansion being carried out under Samuel Daukes. Nesfield was probably introduced to Dudley by Lady Emily Foley, for whom he was designing gardens at Stoke Edith near Hereford. By October 1854, when he came to Witley for three days to discuss the project, Nesfield had established himself as the leading garden designer of his generation and was advising some of the richest landowners in the country; however, he

Above: William Andrews Nesfield in about 1870. He began his career in the army and then as a watercolour painter, but turned to landscape gardening on the advice of his brother-in-law, the architect Anthony Salvin
Below: Witley Court in the 1770s, as portrayed by Edward Dayes. A causeway carries the drive across Front Pool, and 18th-century service blocks flank the main house

Above: W A Nesfield's watercolour of the south parterre, with the fountains playing

Below: The Golden Gates, which once terminated the south parterre, in situ at Witley Court. They can now be found, minus their gilding and some of the more elaborate decoration, in Lake Havasu City, Arizona – the location of the reconstructed London Bridge

was later to refer to the gardens at Witley as his 'monster work'. Like those by Nash and Repton which they replaced, they were intended to provide a suitable setting for the south and east fronts of the mansion and were in a matching Italianate style.

On the south front a flight of steps with curved balustrade connected Nash's portico with the grandiose parterre, which was separated from the deer park beyond by a ha-ha (or concealed ditch) and stone balustrade. From the terrace a broad central gravel walk led down the slope to the quatrefoil-shaped pool at the centre of the parterre, in the middle of which rose the monumental fountain depicting the mythological tale of Perseus and Andromeda. This was designed by Nesfield and installed in 1860. In line with his belief that the immediate setting of a house should be as formal as possible, the gravel walk

was flanked by symmetrical beds of flowers and shrubs outlined with raised stone kerbs (Nesfield preferred these to the usual clipped box if the budget allowed), all embedded in smooth turf. Vertical emphasis was provided by the formal dotting of clipped standard trees. The fountain pool was surrounded by its own symmetrical setting of flower and shrub beds, diversified by standard trees and large flower-filled stone vases or 'tazzas'. A cross-walk ending with ornate stone pavilions (also designed by Nesfield) separated this area from the large semicircular lawn that rose up the far slope, which had its own stone edged parterres and specimen trees and shrubs. Crowning the rise, and terminating the main axis through the garden, were the ornate 'Golden Gates' – not part of Nesfield's original design, but introduced in 1862 in a position where he had intended a belvedere, or viewing platform.

Below the east front was a smaller garden containing a more conventional parterre. This featured all the elements of a 'parterre de broderie', a design of 17th-century French origin which emulates the patterns of embroidery – plant-like motifs of scrolls, volutes and rays, laid out with box and filled in with flowers and coloured gravels. Nesfield's palette for the latter included red (achieved with crushed brick and tile), white (Derbyshire spar) and blue (Westmorland slate). Once again, there were clipped evergreens, ornamental shrubs and tazzas filled with flowers, and a large fountain – the fountain of Flora, goddess of spring – as the centrepiece. At a lower level, between the east and south parterres, was a long flower border designed as a guilloche, or ribbon.

THE LATER VICTORIAN GARDEN

The scale of the Witley gardens, and particularly the fountains, attracted attention from the start, with a succession of gardening correspondents publishing their impressions in various journals. Changing tastes meant that Nesfield's style began to go out of favour in the 1870s. *The Gardeners' Chronicle* in 1872 considered that 'its very magnitude is imposing, but the style of decoration is frittered and childish. It is barbarous in its magnificence, highly irritating and unsatisfactory'. *The Cottage Gardener* in the same year was kinder, conceding that 'embroidered gardens have of late become less fashionable', but concluding that 'here fancy work of this description is so well blended with masses of rhododendrons and other shrubs, which in their turn are enlivened with sculptural objects judiciously placed, that the whole can hardly fail to please the most fastidious'. There is evidence that in the 1880s the internal form and colour of Nesfield's layout began to change as successive head gardeners moved away from the original relatively sophisticated planting, towards the more exuberant bedding-out beloved of later Victorians; one large bed, for instance, contained 5,000 geraniums set off by yellow calceolarias and blue lobelia. It was at this point that the parterres on the south slope were replanted with shrubs to provide a frame for the vista to the Golden Gates. In this period, too, a smaller garden of clipped topiary was laid out (in the former kitchen-garden orchard) to the west of the house for Rachel, the wife of the second earl of Dudley. Meanwhile, the clipped standards in the main parterres continued to grow larger, until they tended to dominate the overall picture when the fountains were not playing. Old photographs and postcards document the gradual evolution of the gardens in these decades.

The 18th-century wilderness and the pools on the north side of the house appear to have been untouched by Nesfield, but in the 1870s and 1880s the valley seems to have been extensively planted with American plants and ornamental trees, together with a profusion of spring-flowering bulbs and plants. Below the dam a footbridge took the ornamental walk across the Shrawley Brook, reinstated in timber and stone in 1999.

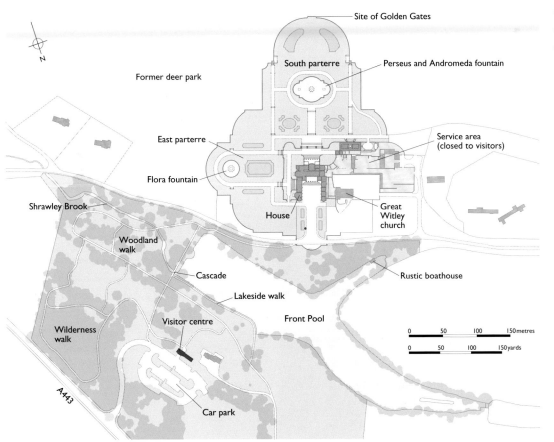

Site of Golden Gates

South parterre

Perseus and Andromeda fountain

Former deer park

East parterre

Service area (closed to visitors)

Flora fountain

Shrawley Brook

House

Great Witley church

Woodland walk

Cascade

Rustic boathouse

Lakeside walk

Front Pool

Wilderness walk

Visitor centre

A443

Car park

Left: A map showing the current extent of the gardens and walks at Witley Court

Below: Witley Court from the south-east. The planting in the restored south parterre incorporates rhododendrons and lavender

THE TWENTIETH-CENTURY GARDEN

A rustic timber boathouse was built on the southern side of the small western arm of Front Pool, probably before 1914, and this was repaired by English Heritage in 1999. On the north side of the pool a stone and brick underground boathouse is set into a steep field-slope. This was used as a punt-house, although its construction date is uncertain.

After 1900 Lord Dudley's deteriorating financial situation (reflecting his lavish spending as well as the declining iron industry) meant that less money was available to keep up the gardens, a situation exacerbated by the First World War and the departure of staff for the Front. The planting of the flower beds was simplified, and photographs taken in 1920 show that, although the lawns continued to be mown, the edges of the beds were not trimmed as they had been. In this state of reduced maintenance the gardens continued

until the disastrous fire of 1937, after which upkeep ceased and the stripping of saleable features began. The Golden Gates, for instance, were sold to Arizona, while offers for the fountains were received at one time or another from Bing Crosby (who wanted them for a golf course at Palm Springs) and Billy Butlin. The stone kerbs around the subsidiary south parterre beds ended up around a war memorial in Stourport-on-Severn, where they remain.

A major sale of standing timber in 1938 resulted in the felling of the majority of the woodland enclosing the park, and few areas were replanted. After the sale of the land between Front Pool and the public road – North Park or Pool House estate – its new private owner planted a screen of conifers which effectively blocked the view of Witley Court from the north.

RESTORATION OF WITLEY'S GARDENS

Since its acquisition by English Heritage in 1996 (with help from the Heritage Lottery Fund), the view of Witley Court from the north has been opened up again and new visitor facilities have been developed in the area. This is also where a new wilderness garden has been created on part of the site of the original wilderness.

Reinstatement of the south parterre began in 2002, and the restored Perseus fountain was 'fired' by HRH the Prince of Wales in November that year. A number of flights of steps have been recreated, using stone from the Forest of Dean to match the original. Gravel paths, grassed over by the Ministry of Works for ease of maintenance, have been relaid. Only the larger flower beds have been restored, given that there are now just four gardeners to keep them up compared with the 24 of Witley's heyday, and inevitably the more labour-intensive elements of Nesfield's scheme have had to be reduced. The scrollwork within them has been made in lavender rather than box, because of the current danger of box blight. The subsidiary beds have been replanted with hybrid rhododendrons, but cost has prevented the missing stone edgings being replaced. Work on the east parterre, including archaeology and restoration of the original planting scheme, began in 2005. It is hoped that at some future date it may be possible to recreate the missing sculptural embellishments of the gardens at Witley.

Victorian Rhododendrons at Witley

Witley Court is home to some extremely unusual varieties of rhododendron, some of which may no longer exist elsewhere. They provide a rare chance to see original Victorian plants lost from other gardens.

Even in the 18th century, new species of plants were being shipped to nurseries and garden owners in England from all over the world. In the 1770s, Loddiges Nursery of Hackney offered *Rhododendron ponticum* (the common mauve rhododendron) for sale, and the popularity of rhododendrons took hold among élite garden owners. Soon after, other species of rhododendron were introduced from North America, the Caucasus mountains and the Himalayas. By the early 19th century, the stage was set for a massive rhododendron breeding programme in which nurseries in Britain tried to 'improve' on nature, making hardier, more reliable and showy plants from these early species.

Victorian gardeners became obsessed by rhododendrons and until the 1860s collections were dominated by hybrids created from these early introductions. Later in the 19th and 20th centuries, further species were introduced, mostly from remote areas of China and the Himalayas, which were again used for hybridization. In most gardens, the early types were replaced with these later hybrids, but at Witley, the rhododendrons that continue to flower in the woodland walks to the north of the house are of the earliest hybrid types, planted between the 1830s and the 1870s. Many of the early types seen at Witley were once common, but have now gone out of general cultivation.

English Heritage is carrying out a survey and research into these old hybrids to understand the original landscape design. The most impressive plants appear to border the pathways – placed to be best admired by visitors. The gardeners at Witley hope to date, identify and label the rhododendrons and to propagate the rarest types to ensure their survival at Witley, and to help restore other gardens where the early types have been lost.

The rhododendrons at Witley Court provide a rare chance to see original Victorian plants lost from other gardens

History of the House

In the 17th century, Witley Court was a modest manor house. By the 19th century it was a vast Italianate estate. The Foleys of Dudley, who made their fortune manufacturing nails, began the expansion, but it was under the earls of Dudley that the estate reached its apogee. With vast wealth from industry, agriculture and plantations in Jamaica, the Dudleys lived on a lavish scale. At Witley Court, they were able to entertain extravagantly, supported by more than 100 servants.

Left: *Detail of a portrait of William Humble Ward, the second earl of Dudley, as governor-general of Australia, painted by Sir John Longstaff in 1914*

Left: This late 17th-century painting, now lost, is the only known view of the Jacobean house at Witley Court, and depicts the south front. The medieval church is shown to the left, and the houses below might be the remains of Witley village, cleared away in the 18th century

Below: A reconstruction drawing of the Jacobean house from the south-east showing it as it appeared in the 17th-century painting. The two towers remained a prominent feature of Witley Court despite later alterations

THE EARLY HOUSE AT WITLEY

Domesday Book of 1086 records the manor of Witley as belonging to Urso d'Abetot, a cousin of William the Conqueror. By the mid-13th century ownership had passed to the Cookseys, a prominent Worcestershire family with estates in the Kidderminster and Bromsgrove areas. The remains of the vaulted chamber which still survives under the entrance hall of the present house probably date from this period or a little later; it might have been the undercroft of a solar, or withdrawing room, at one end of the great hall of the medieval manor house.

On the death of Thomas Cooksey in 1498 Witley descended to his cousin Robert Russell of Strensham. At this stage the manor comprised 120–160ha (300–400 acres), the manor house itself and the adjoining church. Little is known of the substantial new house Russell is said to have built soon after inheriting, although a deer park to the south is thought to have been enclosed in the first half of the 16th century.

Between about 1610 and 1620 the medieval house was rebuilt on a grander scale by a descendant of Robert Russell. Its appearance is recorded by a solitary late 17th-century painting, now lost, of the south front, which shows the central door framed by a pair of massive chimneystacks and short projecting wings. The

main range was crowned by a cupola, and behind rose the twin staircase towers that have remained such a prominent feature of Witley Court ever since. The painting shows large mullion-and-transom windows, with the exception of those on the ends of the wings which were of the so-called 'Ipswich' type. In the foreground were walled enclosures, one of them apparently used as a bowling green. To the left was the medieval church, with a cluster of village houses below. The

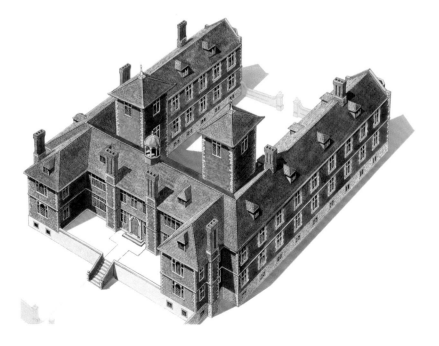

Below: This portrait of Thomas Foley I, the first of eight Thomases to own Witley, commemorates the founding of his charitable school for poor boys. The dedication directs that when they were 'fitt to be Apprentices, care may be taken to place them with such masters as may answer to my Great end, being the Glory of God, & therre Reall Good'

house, which was built of brick with stone dressings, was designed on an H-plan, with long wings projecting on the north, or entrance, front. Of these, the west wing contained a long gallery on the first floor, while the east wing was given over to service accommodation.

During the Civil War, Witley was the residence of Sir William Russell, a royalist supporter, high sheriff of the county and governor of Worcester. In 1652 he is recorded as being threatened with the forfeiture of the estate to Edward Harrison, to whom he was in debt. But the debt must have been paid as, two years later, Sir William gave the property to his son Thomas as a wedding present. In 1655, however, Thomas Russell sold the estate, including the 'impressive residence', to Thomas Foley of Stourbridge.

THOMAS FOLEY, 1617–77

For nearly two centuries Witley was closely associated with the Foley family, whose fortunes were initially based on the iron industry. The foundations were laid in the early 17th century by Richard Foley of Dudley; he began by selling nails, but later became involved in their manufacture as a forge master. Foreign competition was stiff, and he was determined to improve the method by which the nails were made (at that time they were made mainly by hand). He is said to have travelled to Uppsala in Sweden to observe a nail-making machine, which he copied on his return to England. On a further visit to Sweden, for the purposes of what would now be called industrial espionage, he gained entry to the nail works by pretending to be half-witted. He went on to become a rich and respected member of Dudley society, being elected mayor at the age of 36. He married twice, fathering 13 children, and in 1630 moved to Stourbridge, where he had established forges.

His son Thomas (1617–77) further developed the business, doing well out of the Civil War by supplying iron cannons and their ballistics. He married Anne Browne of Spelmonden in Kent, daughter of the greatest gun manufacturer in the country, and inherited a half-share of his father-in-law's business in 1652. This contributed to his reputed annual income of £5,000 – worth about £500,000 in today's money – enabling him to buy the Witley estate. He was highly regarded by contemporaries, enjoying a reputation for 'just and blameless dealing, that all men he ever had to do with ... magnified his great integrity and honesty which was questioned by none'. Like his father, Thomas engaged in local philanthropy, endowing Old Swinford Hospital in Stourbridge, a school for impoverished boys from local parishes, which is still flourishing today. He became high sheriff of Worcestershire in 1655, served as a member of parliament, and died in 1677.

WITLEY IN THE SEVENTEENTH AND EIGHTEENTH CENTURIES

Foley was the first of no fewer than eight Thomases to own the Witley estate. His eldest son (Thomas II, c.1641–1701), who likewise served as high sheriff and an MP, is thought to have carried out substantial work on the house, since

in 1695 it was referred to in William Camden's *Britannia* as 'fair new-built'. It is possible that the work included replacing the original roof with the overhanging hipped roof shown in the early painting. By 1689 he had acquired the six manors that make up Great Witley, totalling about 1,050ha (2,600 acres). His son (Thomas III, 1673–1733), again sheriff and MP, succeeded in 1701 and was created Baron Foley of Kidderminster in 1712. He seems to have begun the process whereby the Foleys gradually abandoned the industrial base which had made them so rich, disposing of many of their ironworks and concentrating instead on being landed aristocracy and politicians. Lord Foley enlarged the house significantly, no doubt intending that it should reflect his enhanced social status, adding an extra floor to the centre block and doubling its depth by filling the space between the existing wings on the south front. Short two-storey wings were added to left and right, and the resulting composition was given central emphasis by a projecting elliptical bow on this side. New parapets were extended around the roof, and bay windows were added to terminate the ends of the north wings. The architect of all these alterations is not known. Lord Foley extended the grounds by acquiring additional land to the north, and planted an imposing avenue on the approach from the east. He had intended to rebuild the medieval church but died before work could begin, so this project fell to his widow and his son Thomas IV (1703–66), the second Lord Foley. The architect of the new church, which was

consecrated in 1735, might have been James Gibbs (1682–1750), better known as the designer of St Martin-in-the-Fields in London, the Radcliffe Camera in Oxford and the Senate House in Cambridge. Gibbs was certainly responsible for installing the windows and ceiling paintings brought from the duke of Chandos's chapel at Canons, Middlesex, in 1747.

Thomas IV continued the transformation by creating a new axial approach from the north, via a causeway across a lake – the Front Pool – formed by damming a stream. The impact of Witley Court on the visitor arriving from the north was enhanced still further by the addition of new service blocks, connected to the house by

Above: An early 19th-century drawing of the north front by George Repton. He shows the bay windows at the ends of the north wings, and the flanking service blocks added in the 18th century

Below: A reconstruction showing Witley Court from the south-east at the time of Repton's drawing. The additional floor and the increase in depth of the centre block of the house can be seen

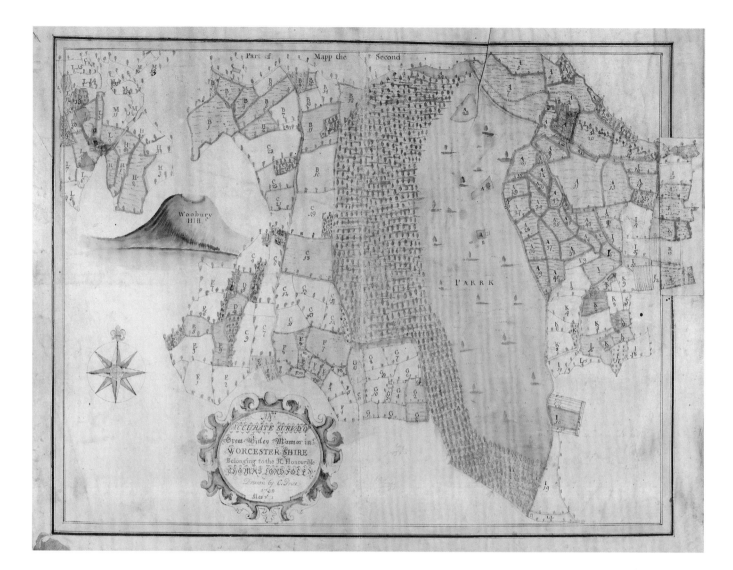

Above: A map by Charles Price of 'Great Witley Manor in Worcestershire, belonging to the Rt Honourable Thomas Lord Foley', 1732. The house and the church can be seen at the top right, with the deer park lying to the west

Right: A watercolour by E F Burney (1760–1848) of Deer Park House, designed by Henry Flitcroft (1697–1769) before 1762. It was demolished in about 1950

curving walls and framed in turn by arcaded screen walls. The result, as recorded in an early 19th-century drawing by George Repton (page 27), must have been extremely impressive. The exact date of these additions is not known, and nor is the identity of the architect; it could have been Gibbs, although another candidate might be the prominent Palladian architect Henry Flitcroft, who at some point before 1762 designed the Keeper's Lodge (also known as Deer Park House) for the second Lord Foley. This not only acted as an eyecatcher in the view from the south side of the house, but also served as a shooting lodge and a home for the head gamekeeper and his family. During the 19th century its handsome portico became a useful grandstand from which sporting events could be viewed. By 1938 this attractive building had become derelict, and in about 1950 it was demolished.

Great Witley Church

The parish church of St Michael and All Angels, although physically attached to the mansion, is the responsibility of the Parochial Church Council rather than English Heritage; it is maintained by the local community. It can be reached by the path from the forecourt.

Witley Church has one of the finest 18th-century ecclesiastical interiors in the country and would be worth a long detour even if Witley Court did not exist. Although at first sight it looks like the private chapel of the house, it has always been the parish church, replacing a ruinous 13th-century building that had stood a little further west. The first Lord Foley planned a new church, which was constructed after his death in 1733 at the expense of his widow, and consecrated in 1735. This had a brick exterior to match the house as it then was, and a plain interior; the architect might have been James Gibbs.

Twelve years later the church was transformed when the second Lord Foley bought some of the fittings from the recently demolished chapel of the duke of Chandos's mansion at Canons, Edgware (Middlesex). This too, one of the most magnificent baroque interiors of its day, had originally been designed by Gibbs, who was brought in again to fit out the Witley interior, incorporating ceiling panels painted by Antonio Bellucci and ten windows painted by the London glass-painter Joshua Price after designs by Francesco Sleter. Gibbs provided a design for an elaborate new vaulted ceiling, carried out not in the usual plaster but in papier mâché (then a recent invention) by Thomas Bromwich of Ludgate Hill, London, who probably added some of the rococo embellishments. Bellucci's paintings include the big central oval of the Ascension and smaller panels of cherubs with symbols of the Passion, while Price's windows depict scenes from the life of Christ.

The transepts to either side of the altar contain Foley family monuments. To the left is a handsome pedimented tablet to Thomas Foley I (died 1677), saved from the medieval church, while to the right is the vast pyramidal composition commemorating the first Lord Foley and his family. This was designed and carved in 1753 by Michael Rysbrack

(1694–1770), perhaps the leading sculptor of his generation in England, whose incised signature can be found on the monument. It cost £2,000 – more than £200,000 today. Most of the other fittings of the church – pews, pulpit, font – were introduced by Samuel Daukes for the first earl of Dudley in 1861, replacing existing Georgian fittings which were then exiled to Fawley church near Henley-on-Thames. Daukes was also responsible for encasing the brick exterior in stone, so that it matched the newly encased mansion. In 1913 mosaics by Salviati & Co were incorporated into the reredos behind the altar.

The church was happily untouched by the fire but with the decline of the house into ruin it too became sadly neglected. Restoration began in 1965 on the initiative of the parishioners and between 1993 and 1994 the whole of the interior, including Bellucci's panels, was cleaned.

Witley Church has one of the finest 18th-century ecclesiastical interiors in the country

Below: The magnificent interior of Witley Church incorporates ceiling panels by Italian artist Antonio Bellucci (1654–1726), and painted glass by Joshua Price of London (1672–1722)

Above: Lady Harriet Foley, the wife of 'Lord Balloon'. In 1776 a contemporary reported that, as a result of her husband's debts, it was 'thought a good joke that Lady H F was handed out of her own house into her coach by two bailyfs' having had her jewels and clothes seized
Right: An engraving of 1784 entitled All On Fire, *recording the failed ascent of Allen Keegan's balloon from the grounds of Foley House, London, on 20 September that year. The balloon caught fire and the gantry collapsed*

Facing page top: Cockerell's sketches and notes of Witley Court in 1821, showing the use of the principal rooms after John Nash's remodelling
Facing page bottom: A reconstruction drawing showing Witley Court from the south-east, as remodelled in the 19th century. The massive portico and small conservatory added by Nash on the south side of the house can be seen, but the flanking service blocks to the north have been removed

When the second Lord Foley died a bachelor in 1766 the title became extinct and the estate passed to his second cousin, Thomas V (1716–77), of Stoke Edith near Hereford. He, too, continued the family tradition of parliamentary service, and in 1776 was elevated to the peerage as Baron Foley of the second creation. His two elder sons got into debt and were a great disappointment to him. The successor to his title, Thomas VI (1742–93), was dubbed 'Lord Balloon' after an incident in which a hot-air balloon got out of control in the gardens of his London house. He achieved high office as a privy councillor and lord lieutenant of Worcestershire, but the contemporary Royal Register noted that he had also, 'by a most rapid course of debauchery, extravagance and gambling, involved himself in a state of distress from the misery and disgrace of which he can never be extricated'. As a result of his behaviour he was disinherited by his father, and under him the family fortune was badly eroded.

NINETEENTH-CENTURY ALTERATIONS

Thomas VII (1780–1833), the third and only surviving son of Thomas VI, succeeded his profligate father in 1793, aged only 13. In 1806 he was able to restore his financial position by marrying a daughter of the second duke of Leinster, Ireland's premier peer. This may have enabled him to commission John Nash (1752–1835), the leading Regency architect, to design a succession of ambitious alterations to Witley. Nash was on friendly terms with the family, staying frequently at Witley over the years.

His work here is difficult to date precisely, but it included the addition of the massive stone porticos to the north and south fronts (that on the north seems to have come first, being referred to in print in 1814); the raising of the wings so that the roof-line corresponded with the cornice on the porticos; and rebuilding the roof to a flatter pitch with overhanging 'Tuscan' eaves. It is possible that he was responsible for the application of a coat of white stucco to the whole exterior to mask the successive alterations of two centuries, except that a drawing of about 1800 appears to show the house already stuccoed. The interior was replanned around the central gallery that Nash favoured in large houses, and the east wing was rebuilt. Here Nash created a sequence of rooms, including a dining room and library, which are known only through notes made by the great neoclassical architect C R Cockerell when he visited Witley in December 1821. Cockerell, who generally disapproved of Nash's work, described these interiors as 'red Etruscan, &

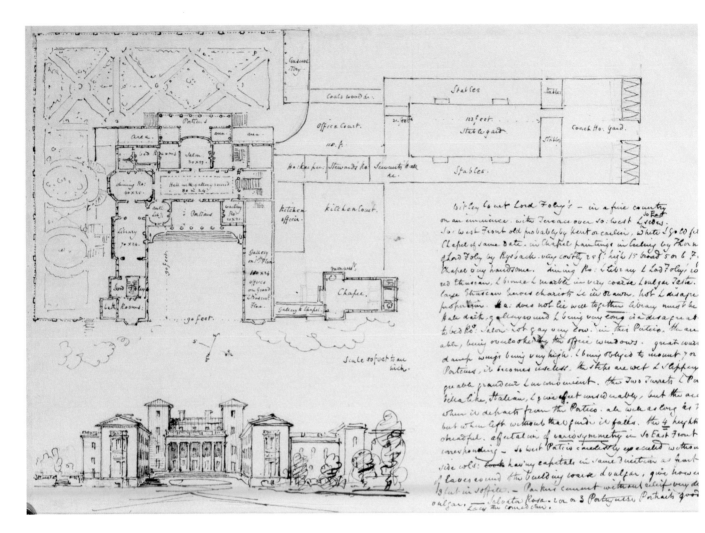

bronze & marble in very coarse & vulgar taste, coved rooms with large Etruscan heroes, chariots etc ill drawn, hot & disagreeable in color & proportion'. In reality Nash's interiors were probably good and characteristic examples of the sumptuous Regency taste which he had used elsewhere, above all for the Prince Regent at Carlton House and subsequently at Buckingham Palace. He also demolished the service blocks on the north front and replaced them with new accommodation around two courtyards at the south-west corner of the house. Finally, in 1828, George Repton (architect son of the celebrated landscape gardener Humphry Repton, and Nash's one-time assistant) built kennels to house Lord Foley's pack of hounds, designed as interlocking octagonal pavilions and exercise yards; these stood in the park well to the west of the mansion. Humphry Repton himself appears to have been consulted on the landscaping, although no documentation survives.

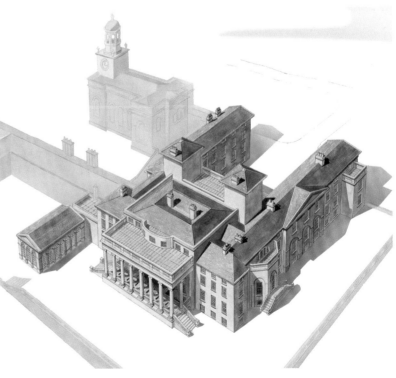

Right: The earl of Dudley's Round Oak Iron and Steel Works at Brierley Hill, as shown in an engraved advertisement of between 1890 and 1894. The earls of Dudley owned Witley Court from 1837. The earl's cable works, another of his enterprises, is labelled in the distance on the left

Below: This photograph of 1898 shows a full complement of men employed at one of Lord Dudley's forges – from young apprentices to office clerks and furnacemen

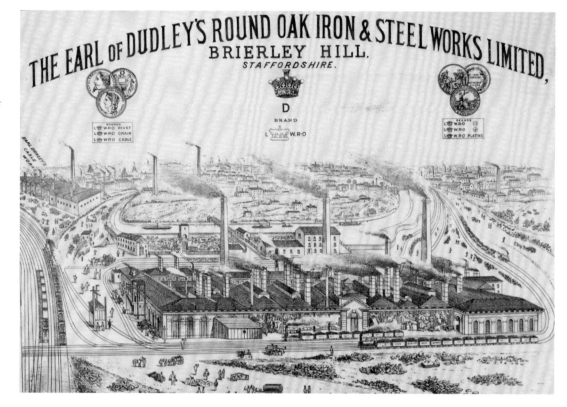

Despite his advantageous marriage, in 1810 Lord Foley was forced to raise a loan of £24,000 from Nash on the security of Foley House in London, although in 1812 the architect is said to have paid him the sum of £70,000 (about £2.4 million today) for the house, which stood in the way of the new street Nash was creating between Regent's Park and Carlton House in Pall Mall. Nevertheless, within four years of Foley's death in 1833, his son, Thomas VIII (1808–69) was obliged to sell the Witley estate for £900,000 (equivalent to about £48 million today) to the trustees of William Ward, so bringing the long Foley connection to an end.

WITLEY'S VICTORIAN HEYDAY

In 1837 the new owner of Witley, William Ward (1817–85), 11th Baron Ward of Birmingham, was still a minor. Even so, he was one of the richest individuals in England. As with the Foleys, the wealth was based on West Midlands industry, but in this case from the technical innovations of the Industrial Revolution. He was heir to the income from more than 200 mines in the Black Country, from which were extracted coal, iron, limestone and fireclay. He also owned iron-smelting works, chemical factories and a railway construction business, which together generated an annual income of some £100,000 (over £5 million today). Ward had inherited these vast assets in 1833 from a distant relation, John William Ward (1781–1833), first earl of Dudley and a former foreign secretary. The latter was known as 'the Lorenzo of the Black Country', presumably in reference to Lorenzo de Medici, ruler of Florence at the height of the Renaissance and renowned as a great patron of the arts.

The Dudleys' Industrial Enterprises

The great wealth of the Ward family, earls of Dudley, who owned Witley Court between 1837 and 1920, derived from a number of sources, primarily landed estates, industrial enterprises and plantations in Jamaica. In 1883 William Ward, first earl of Dudley of the second creation, was noted as owning a total of 25,000 acres in England and Wales – over 14,000 in Worcestershire, nearly 5,000 in Staffordshire, and over 4,000 in Wales. The vast annual income of £123,000 that these generated arose partly from agriculture and rents but far more from the industrial activities that took place on them.

The south Staffordshire properties were the most lucrative, with their coal mines and associated products, together with iron-smelting works, chemical factories and a railway construction business. The development of the area had in fact been spearheaded by John, second viscount Dudley and Ward, after he inherited his title in 1774. He enlarged existing mineral and iron works into a major centre of production, made possible by recent technological advances in iron production (notably blast furnaces fired by local coal rather than charcoal). Using his own capital and his position as MP and lord of the manor to take the lead, he promoted the construction of the Stourbridge and Dudley Canals (the latter passing

through his largest colliery), linking Birmingham and the Black Country to the river Severn, and facilitating the transport of heavy materials. By the mid-19th century the earl of Dudley's vast Round Oak Ironworks (later Round Oak Steelworks) at Brierley Hill was served not only by a branch of the Great Western Railway but also by Lord Dudley's own Pensnett railway. This had nearly 40 miles of single track, servicing the earl's industrial enterprises in the area as well as those of other companies.

The third main element in the Dudley portfolio comprised plantations in Jamaica. The principal one was the Whitney estate of over 1,200ha (3,000 acres), at Clarendon on the edge of the Mocho Mountains, which came into the Ward family through marriage to an heiress of the Carver family, descendants of the original settler. Renowned for its fertile soil, it grew coffee, sugar cane, bananas and cocoa, as well as other agricultural products. Sixty-four hectares (158 acres) were given over to sugar cane, which was processed in a water mill to produce sugar and rum. The mill was fed by an aqueduct (shown in James Hakewill's view of 1825 below) and supplemented by steam power, until sugar production was abandoned in the 1880s. Immediately before the abolition of the transatlantic slave trade in 1807, the estate was recorded as being worked by 270 slaves.

Coffee, sugar cane, bananas and cocoa grown on the fertile soils of their Jamaican estates contributed to the immense wealth of the Ward family

Above: John William Ward, third viscount Dudley and Ward and first earl of Dudley, inherited industrial estates in the Black Country and abroad on the death of his father, the second viscount, also named John, in 1823
Left: The Whitney estate, owned by the earls of Dudley, by James Hakewill in his 'Picturesque Tour in the Island of Jamaica', 1825. The curving wall carried an aqueduct to the industrial buildings in the distance

Right: William Ward, first earl of Dudley of the second creation, for whom Witley Court and its gardens were completely remodelled; a photograph taken in the 1860s

Right: William Ward, first earl of Dudley of the second creation, for whom Witley Court and its gardens were completely remodelled; a photograph taken in the 1860s

The earl died insane, conversing with himself in two voices, one falsetto and one bass.

Young Lord Ward did not come into his full inheritance until the age of 28, and meanwhile he lived at the family home of Himley Hall, near Stourbridge. After necessary repairs Witley Court was let, most notably between 1843 and 1846 to Queen Adelaide, widow of King William IV. She was a popular figure locally, paying for the building of the first village school and often seen out and about in her carriage. After her departure Lord Ward moved in. In 1851 he married a society beauty, Selina Constance de Burgh, but she died in childbirth the same year. Soon afterwards, perhaps as a way of mitigating his grief, Ward began to

plan a major transformation of Witley Court and its surroundings, which was duly carried out between 1854 and 1860.

LORD WARD'S TRANSFORMATION OF WITLEY COURT

The simple, even austere, neoclassical idiom which Nash had used on the exterior was already out of fashion, and so Ward now commissioned the architect Samuel Whitfield Daukes (1811–80) to remodel the house in the more ornate Italianate style used between 1845 and 1848 for the creation of Osborne House on the Isle of Wight for Queen Victoria. Daukes was not a particularly well-known architect; he had trained in York before

Left: The remodelled Witley Court and the south parterre shown soon after completion in a lithograph of 1879. The balustrade separated the formal gardens from the surrounding deer park

Below: A reconstruction drawing showing Witley Court from the south-east following Samuel Daukes's final modifications in the late 1850s. He remodelled the house in an ornate Italian style and added the curved wing and enormous conservatory to the south-west of the house

starting a practice in Gloucester in 1837, where he became the architect of the railway linking the city with Birmingham. He had, however, proved his familiarity with the Italianate style in his rebuilding of Abberley Hall near Witley from 1845 to 1846. No doubt it was this local connection that drew him to Lord Ward's attention.

The transformation of Witley involved the recasting of the entire exterior (including the adjoining church) in Bath stone to match Nash's porticos, which were the only existing features left untouched. Yet again the house was re-roofed, this time with a flat-pitched lead roof concealed by a balustraded parapet. A new curving wing was added at the south-west corner, leading to an enormous glass-roofed conservatory which replaced the more modest one added by Nash. Elaborate gardens were designed by W A Nesfield at that time (see pages 19–20). Inside the house the Georgian interiors gave way to a fashionable cosmetic modernization, grafted onto existing walls and designed by Moxons, the royal decorators. Extensive use was made of mouldings in carton pierre. Although the entrance hall was relatively restrained, the main reception rooms, including the vast ballroom, were in variations of the white-and-gold 'Tous les Louis' decoration (inspired by French interiors of the reigns of Louis XIV and XV) much favoured by the

fashionable English élite at that time. Many of the marble chimneypieces and other embellishments were carved by James Forsyth, designer of the Perseus and Andromeda fountain. In the east wing Daukes installed a so-called fireproof floor of steel girders and concrete – probably intended as much as anything to support the additional weight created by the stone-cladding – which was to prove completely ineffective in the 1937 fire.

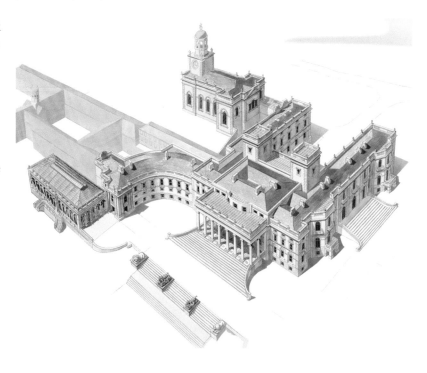

21st Birthday Celebrations

There was a full-scale fair with merry-go-rounds and Punch and Judy shows. An elaborate fireworks display rounded off the evening

The celebrations for the young second earl's coming-of-age in 1888 were spread over three days. On 7 August he and his mother received congratulatory deputations from the tenants of the Witley Court and Holt estates, and in the evening there was a splendid ball for the county, attended by 214 guests, held in a large marquee. Another marquee accommodated the guests' coachmen, while a huge temporary stable was provided for 100 horses.

The next day there were congratulations from deputations of tradesmen (both local and from London), presented in the picture gallery, while the third day was given over to entertaining the tenantry on a grand scale. An even larger marquee, over 60m long, was erected in the park, in which 900 male cottagers sat down to an ample lunch washed down with beer. There was also a full-scale fair, complete with merry-go-rounds and Punch and Judy shows. Pleasure boats floated on the Front Pool, the drives were decorated with flags and bunting, and the fountains played for an hour. Tea was served to 416 children and 427 village women, followed by dancing to the accompaniment of two bands. As dusk fell the fountains were illuminated, and an elaborate fireworks display rounded off the evening.

Right: William Humble Ward, second earl of Dudley, as a young man

THE EARLS OF DUDLEY AT WITLEY

In 1860, the year that the transformation was completed, the earldom of Dudley was revived and conferred on Lord Ward in recognition of his generosity to local charities (as well, no doubt, as his immense wealth). In 1865 he married Georgina Elizabeth Moncrieffe, a lady of 'peerless' beauty, with whom he had six sons and one daughter. The earl died in 1885 at the age of 67 (he is buried at Witley but his monument is in Worcester Cathedral, whose restoration he helped fund), but his widow survived until 1929, famous locally for her stately bearing, good looks and charm. Their son the second earl (also named William) inherited aged 18 and did not take up residence at Witley until he was 21, when there were lavish festivities lasting three days. These were repeated in 1891 when he married Rachel Anne Gurney, a Norfolk banking heiress who was later described as having 'the beauty of an eastern queen'.

At the height of the family's prosperity the Dudleys owned properties and estates in London (Dudley House and 7 Carlton Gardens), Cheshire, Scotland, Wales, Ireland, Boulogne, Nice, Rome,

Vienna and Jamaica. By 1883 the English and Welsh estates totalled 10,300ha (25,554 acres), of which more than 5,700ha (14,000 acres) were in Worcestershire. Thanks to the extensive coal mines on them, the annual income from them was about £123,000 (about £7 million today), a sum exceeded by only six other noblemen in the country. Life at Witley was correspondingly opulent, and reached a zenith during the 1890s, when the second earl's friend the prince of Wales (later King Edward VII) became a regular visitor. He and his entourage were attracted particularly by Lord Dudley's elaborate shooting parties. The park had a staff of 25 full-time gamekeepers who maintained a stock of partridges, pheasants and deer for these occasions. A frequent house guest, Mrs Berkeley, who as a young woman was often invited to Witley Court, later recalled, 'One side of the gay life I loathed, the game question. The battues, the wholesale slaughter of tame birds driven into a corner, the crowd of keepers, the destroyed crops, the ravaged pasture land, and what all these things meant to the farmers on the estate'. In 1895, a golf course was laid out for the further entertainment of guests.

During the grand house parties the house would be full with family, staff and guests. The latter would stay for up to a week, bringing with them their own servants, who also had to be accommodated – a valet for each gentleman and a personal maid for each lady to organize their frequent changes of clothing during the day. Some guests even brought their own cook. The prince of Wales, often travelling without his wife Princess Alexandra, had a large retinue which might include his personal loaders for the shooting. A day of sporting activities created substantial appetites, which were gratified by enormous dinners, held, when numbers required, in the ballroom or picture gallery.

This lifestyle was supported by a permanent staff of servants, presided over by the butler. He was in charge of the indoor male staff and responsible for the service of meals, drinks and the smooth running of the household generally. The housekeeper took her orders from the countess and, via an army of housemaids, dealt with all cleaning duties. Of equal rank were the head cook and head gardener, each of whom had a large staff that brought the total to over 100.

Above: The prince of Wales and the earl and countess of Dudley in front of the north portico, December 1884, with servants in attendance. The large bronze lion sculptures were later moved to the steps of the south portico
Below: Rachel in 1908, in her robes as countess of Dudley

Facing page top: A portrait of Georgina, countess of Dudley

Right: A royal shooting party in the deer park at Witley, 8 December 1892. The prince of Wales stands in the centre; to the left are the second earl (in the white waistcoat and cap) and his first wife Rachel
Below: Gertie Millar, the second wife of the second earl of Dudley in a postcard from about 1905

Facing page top: Sir Herbert 'Piggy' Smith, owner of Witley, in about 1920

THE END OF AN ERA

As a result of his wealth and connections, the second earl was appointed to a succession of public offices, including lord lieutenant of Ireland (1902–5), privy councillor and, finally, governor-general of Australia (1908–11), all of which would have involved him in considerable personal expense. Although he and his wife had seven children, born between 1892 and 1907, they were very different people, with different attitudes to life. While Lord Dudley was gregarious and a central figure in the prince of Wales's racy circle, Lady Dudley's values were for duty, home, family and church, and she was much given to good works. Eventually cracks began to appear in the marriage and in 1908 a legal separation was agreed, with Witley Court settled on the countess. She took a great interest in the gardens, laying out an area with clipped topiary known as 'My Lady's Garden' which is now the garden of the church tearooms. On Sunday mornings she would lead her staff in a stately procession through the house to church.

Meanwhile, partly as a result of foreign competition, the Dudley wealth was on the wane. It is said that the foot of the main staircase at Witley was flanked by two large wooden urns, which were later found to be full of unpaid bills, tossed there by Lord Dudley on his way down to breakfast each morning. Between 1889 and 1913 the earl is known to have mortgaged the estate and sold pictures to fund his extravagant entertaining. When Lady Dudley was drowned in a swimming accident at the family house in County Galway in 1920, he immediately decided to sell the Witley estate. In 1924 he married his second wife, a former Gaiety girl named Gertie Millar, moved back to the family home, Himley Hall and died in 1932. The Dudley family line continues, even though its connection with Witley has long ceased.

BASSANO
11538 C   MISS GERTIE MILLAR.   ROTARY PHOTO. E.C.

THE FINAL YEARS

The new owner in 1920 was another rich industrialist aspiring to the status of landed gentry, the carpet manufacturer Sir Herbert Smith (1872–1943). Born in Kidderminster in 1872, Smith worked his way up through the ailing carpet manufacturer Humphries, becoming general manager in 1906 and, after turning the company's finances around, buying it in 1910. In 1920 he set up a conglomerate, Carpet Trades Ltd, receiving a baronetcy in the same year (for services as chairman of the Carpet Rationing Committee in the First World War) and retiring a millionaire two years later, aged 49. Although his corpulent physique earned him the unflattering nickname 'Piggy', he came from a musical family and was an accomplished violinist. He acquired Witley Court furnished but, although he expended money in installing electricity, he also reduced staff levels (to just half-a-dozen maids and a butler) and retreated to the south-west corner, effectively abandoning parts of the house. Its existence as a rich man's home was brought to an abrupt end by the devastating fire which broke out at about 8pm on 7 September 1937, while Sir Herbert was away. Starting, it would seem, in the bakery in the basement of the south-east corner of the house and fanned by a strong wind, the fire spread rapidly to the main rooms. Little could be done to quell

Living on the Estate

Mrs Lorna Harrold (1918–2008) lived on the Witley estate until 1924, when she was six:

'When Sir Herbert Smith took the Court over he let us live in the Park House in the deer park, because we were such a big family – 10 together with me. When the Dudleys lived at the Court, it was an overflow for the guests and their servants when they were having a big do. There were stables attached and the house was covered in yellow tea roses. Inside there were beautiful ornate ceilings. It was a lovely place.

'My father was head groom to Lord and Lady Dudley and he used to go hunting with the hounds. My stepsisters and brothers pretty well all worked at the Court. One of my brothers was under-chauffeur and one was a cook. Anybody from the village who left school was almost certain of a job there. They had huge gardens and employed a lot of gardeners. My brother Ben was a gardener there. In the summer he had to mow the lawns. A little bay pony called Kitty pulled the mower and he had to fit her with leather boots to stop her hooves marking the grass.

'After Lady Dudley died Sir Herbert Smith bought the Court. He used to have a big Rolls Royce and he would go through the village every day in his top hat. He had a lot of money, but he wasn't a gentleman.'

'Anybody from the village who left school was almost certain of a job there – my stepsisters and brothers pretty well all worked at the Court'

Below: Lorna Harrold (née Cooper) with some of her brothers and sisters at Witley in 1921. In the back row, from left to right, are Mary, Hilda, Cecil, Frank and Bessie. In the front row are John (sitting) and Lorna (standing)

the flames since the hydrant system connected to the fountain reservoir had not been maintained and Daukes's 'fireproof' floors proved useless. Only a handful of staff were in the building, and, although with the help of villagers many of the contents were saved, the central and eastern sections were gutted. It was, wrote a reporter from a local paper, 'a fine but awful spectacle'. When it turned out that insurance money would pay for no more than a quarter of the cost of rebuilding, Smith decided to dispose of the property. No one was ever to live in the house again. The surviving contents and many garden ornaments were auctioned over eight days in the autumn of 1938, followed by the sale of the house itself the following year to a Mr Banks for a mere £4,000 (about £150,000). The land was sold off separately for agriculture, and standing timber was felled.

RUIN AND RESURRECTION

Witley Court changed hands again in 1954, when it was bought by an antique dealer from Stratford-upon-Avon who stripped and sold anything of value that remained – marble chimneypieces from the ravaged interior, lead, slates and timber from the roof, statuary from the garden and heavy plate-glass from the conservatory. Ruin rapidly overtook the structure, with trees growing up through the floors, and in the 1950s and 1960s it narrowly survived demolition and associated proposals for a motor-racing circuit, caravan park and housing estate. The church might have been bodily removed to London, while the Perseus and Andromeda fountain nearly ended up on a traffic island outside Worcester Cathedral. A Building Preservation Order, however, provided vital protection in 1964, and in 1970 the house and surroundings were scheduled as an Ancient Monument. Once the Department of the Environment had served a compulsory guardianship order in 1972, work to arrest further decay could begin – a task continued since 1984 by English Heritage.